Elgin Cathedral

Richard Fawcett
Principal Inspector of Ancient Monuments

*My church was the ornament of the realm,
the glory of the kingdom,
the delight of foreigners and stranger guests*

Alexander Bur *(bishop of Moray 1362-1397)*

EDINBURGH: HMSO

Introduction

Elgin Cathedral is one of the most beautiful of Scotland's ruined medieval churches and it is hardly surprising that it has provided inspiration for artists over at least two centuries. It also has a great deal to offer to those with an interest in historic architecture, and its intriguingly complex building history well repays closer consideration.

The first phase of the building's history began around 1224, when the pope gave his permission to fix the cathedral at Elgin. Before that it had been variously at Birnie, Spynie and Kinneddar. This first building on the site at Elgin was a cross-shaped structure with a tower at the crossing and eventually with two other towers flanking the great processional entrance at the west end.

After a fire in 1270 the opportunity was taken to extend the building on a large scale. Aisles and chapels were added and the eastern limb was lengthened, presumably to give more space to the high altar and the seating of its principal clergy, the canons. An octagonal chapter-house was also added on the north side of the choir as a meeting room for the canons.

By the end of the thirteenth century the cathedral had reached its full size. But there was further rebuilding after it was set on fire in 1390 by the earl of Buchan (known as the "Wolf of Badenoch"), who had a score to settle with the bishop. The repairs dragged on for over a century and may not have been

An aerial view of the cathedral from the south-west.

The west front, with John Shanks in the left foreground (from A Series of Views ... of Elgin Cathedral, 1826).

fully completed before the Reformation of 1560 left the cathedral redundant.

For the following two and a half centuries the cathedral was little more than a quarry for building materials, although towards the end of that period many people were coming to appreciate its beauty. Largely due to the single-handed efforts of John Shanks, who was appointed first keeper of the ruins in 1807, it was cleared of collapsed masonry, and its surviving glories were fully exposed to view. At the same time it was realised that the State, as nominal owner of the cathedral from the late seventeenth century, should be responsible for its upkeep. It is now cared for by Historic Scotland, the successor of the nineteenth-century Office of Works.

The Earlier Cathedrals

David I (on the left), from a charter of Kelso Abbey. (Reproduced by kind permission of the Duke of Roxburghe)

Early Moray

The name Moray was originally used to describe those parts of Scotland beyond the mountain chain of the Mounth that were occupied by the northern Picts. The virtually independent rulers of this area were sometimes referred to as kings in their own right, though they were later thought of less grandly as mormaers (or stewards).

From perhaps as early as the eleventh century, these mormaers may have appointed a bishop to govern the Church in their territory, in the same way that the kings of Scotland were beginning to introduce bishops into the territories over which they exercised effective control. Although there can be no certainty in this, it is significant that the first bishop of whom we hear, about 1114, has a name which suggests that he may have been of native stock. This name was Gregory, which is probably a latinised version of Giric.

David I and Moray

There was frequent friction between the Scottish kings and Moray, except for a period between 1040 and 1057 when Macbeth, who had been ruler of Moray, became king of the whole country. It was only in the reign of David I (1124-53) that the beginnings of a permanent solution were found, following a major rising in 1130.

As a younger son with little prospect of succeeding to the Scottish throne, David had been sent in his youth to live in England, where his sister was to marry King Henry I in 1100. There he eventually married a wealthy heiress and was granted vast estates. From his years as an English courtier and land-holder, David gained first-hand experience of the ways in which the Anglo-Norman kings established their control over the outlying parts of their kingdom, and when he succeeded to the Scottish crown he set about doing much the same in his own kingdom.

After 1130, he established in Moray an administrative system in which Elgin, Forres and Inverness became the centres from which the area was governed, each with its own burgh and castle. Elgin itself was a burgh by as early as 1136, and eventually had a sheriff as the principal royal officer. One result of this subdivison was that the name Moray came to mean little more than the sub-district centred on Elgin, although the diocese continued to cover a larger area. David also introduced newcomers into the area to hold lands directly from himself and govern them on the feudal principles that he was introducing elsewhere in Scotland. One of these, called Freskin, was probably originally from Flanders; he was granted the lands of Duffus and was to be the ancestor of the powerful de Moravia family.

The diocese of Moray,

The Church was to play an important part in David I's plans for Moray, since its carefully structured organisation was as effective a tool for introducing order as were the secular institutions. Monasteries were established for the Benedictine order at Urquhart, some time between 1130 and 1150, and for the Cistercians at Kinloss in 1150. Bishops with Norman-sounding names began to be appointed, whose loyalties were perhaps clearer than those appointed by the mormaers. The first of these was William, elected in 1152 or 1153.

The early bishops of Moray had their see based at various times at Kinneddar, Birnie and Spynie. It was only after 7 April 1206, when papal permission was granted to Bishop Brice de Douglas (1203-22), that it was fixed at the last of those; the move took place some time between March 1207 and June 1208. Kinneddar and Birnie had been centres of early Christianity, and carved stones produced between the seventh and ninth centuries have been found at both. Birnie also has a handsome small church of the first half of the twelfth century, the architectural details of which show Anglo-Norman influence, presumably as a result of David I's policies. This church was probably used as one of their cathedrals by the earlier bishops.

A figure of St Andrew from the cap of the central pier in the chapter-house.

A map of the area of Moray around Elgin surveyed by Timothy Pont in the late 16th century and published in Blaeu's Atlas novus *dated 1654. (Reproduced by kind permission of the Trustees of the National Library of Scotland).*

The cathedral at Spynie

Scottish cathedrals at this time were not necessarily vast buildings, and it is unlikely that the cathedral which Brice erected at Spynie was large. It may have been embodied in the church which survived until 1735, when the decision was taken to rebuild the parish church elsewhere. The last surviving part of this building stood until about 1850, although as late as 1924 foundations of a simple structure of 22.5 by 10.7 m (74 x 35 ft) were said to be still visible.

A cathedral had to have a chapter of clergy, both to conduct the services which reflected its dignity as the major church of the diocese and to administer its possessions. At first this chapter may have been formed by gatherings of the clergy of the churches within the diocese, since references to the archdeacon (an officer in charge of the parish clergy) seem to suggest that he was more important than the dean (the principal cathedral dignitary). However, the papal permission for the establishment of the see at Spynie also authorised the organisation of a chapter of eight canons. These included the dignitaries of dean, chanter or precentor (responsible for the music of the services), treasurer (in charge of the cathedral's precious possessions), chancellor (businessman and lawyer to the chapter) and archdeacon. Each of these officers was supported by a salary known as a prebend, drawn largely from the incomes originally provided for parish churches which were appropriated for this purpose. The model adopted for the cathedral's constitution was that of the cathedral of Lincoln; indeed, the earliest surviving account of Lincoln's constitution is the one sent for guidance to Spynie.

The churches of Kinneddar (King Edward) Birnie (see below) and Spynie may originally have served as the first cathedrals of the diocese of Moray.

The First Cathedral at Elgin

Spynie Palace, from the shore of the loch.

The move to Elgin

The reason given for fixing the see at Spynie was that up to that time the cathedral had been in an inaccessible angle of the sea, presumably a reference to Kinneddar. But Spynie was itself soon found to be inconvenient, apparently because it was exposed to warfare. Since Elgin was already established as the secular administrative centre of the area, however, it may be that it was seen as appropriate in any case that the Church should be administered from the same centre (though this was not usually the case elsewhere). On 10 April 1224 the pope gave permission for the see to be moved to Elgin, and this was accomplished soon afterwards in the time of Bishop Andrew, a member of the de Moravia family. Nevertheless, the bishops continued to live at one or other of the old bases of the see, and Spynie Castle, or Palace, eventually established itself as their principal residence.

By this time Scottish cathedrals were becoming more expressive of the importance of their bishops, both in their buildings and in their liturgical life. Like the monasteries, they provided a setting for a perpetual round of prayer in which the ordinary folk normally played little part. At Elgin the lay folk of the area had even less of a place in the cathedral than was usual in Scotland, since they had their own parish church of St Giles at the centre of the burgh. Nevertheless, many people would go to the cathedral on major festivals, though space was provided for them in a different part of the building from that occupied by the main body of cathedral clergy.

In keeping with the more expansive ideas of what a cathedral should be, Bishop Andrew increased the chapter of canons or prebendaries from eight to eighteen in 1226. It was further increased to twenty-three before his death in 1242, and only two more canons were to be added to this number before the end of the Middle Ages. Since a cathedral chapter might sometimes be at odds with its bishop, arrangements were made at Elgin for the bishop to be a member of the chapter by granting him the prebend of Forres.

The medieval parish church of St Giles, before its reconstruction in 1827-8.

Although the ideal of a cathedral foundation was that all of its canons and dignitaries should be present to sing the daily services, this was seldom possible. Many had occupations which prevented them from spending all (or in some cases any) of their time at the cathedral, though in 1240 it was decided that non-residents should be fined by losing one seventh of their income. Perhaps such absenteeism was inevitable at a period when one of the few ways in which a monarch could pay his principal officers was to grant them some high church office. To ensure the maintenance of the unbroken round of services Bishop Andrew made provision for seventeen substitute clergy, known as vicars choral, of whom seven were full priests and the others deacons or sub-deacons. Most of the canons and dignitaries were provided with manses in the chanonry or close which grew up around the cathedral.

The first cathedral church at Elgin

Like Birnie and Kinneddar, Elgin seems to have been a centre of the early Church. But early Christian activity there was probably focused on the site eventually occupied by the parish church, in the centre of the medieval burgh rather than on the later cathedral site. It was near the parish church, for instance, that the splendid cross slab decorated with Pictish symbols, now displayed within the cathedral, was found in 1823. Nevertheless, the terms of the permission given for the move in 1224 might suggest that a church dedicated to the Holy Trinity already existed on the land which had been granted for the new cathedral by King Alexander II. The explanation of this may be that work had already started on the cathedral itself a little time before formal permission for the move was received.

On the architectural evidence, the new cathedral was a cross-shaped building, smaller than what we now see. It had a rectangular eastern limb, probably corresponding to the first three bays of the later building, but without flanking aisles. This part contained the presbytery area around the high altar, and the choir of the canons and vicars, whose stalls would have extended down the flanks. Projecting from each side of this was a cross arm known as a transept, which provided space for additional altars. Above the crossing at the junction of the choir and transepts would have risen a central tower, possibly intended to contain bells in its upper stage. To the west of the transepts was the part of the cathedral that was open to lay folk and was known as the nave. Since the decision to build two western towers seems to have been taken after work had started, it is likely that the first nave was just six bays long. It was flanked on each side by an aisle. A plan can be found inside the back cover.

The Pictish cross-slab, possibly carved in the ninth century and found near the parish church in 1823. This face shows a hunting scene and Pictish symbols.

The south transept, seen from the outside.

The architecture of the first cathedral

Although this first building was extensively altered at later stages of its history, and much of what was left has in any case been destroyed, there are still many clues to its original appearance. It is possible that some of the work may have been the responsibility of the master mason named Gregory who is referred to in the bishops' Register.

The presbytery and choir, as the liturgically most important parts of the building, would have been the first to be built, and a considerable length of their north wall still survives. From this it seems that the first eastern limb was lower than the rest of the building. Faint traces of arches, still visible below the clearstorey (upper rank of windows) that was later added above it, suggest that its walls were decorated by a series of arches pierced at intervals by windows above the level of the canons' stalls.

The south transept, interior.

The most complete part of the first cathedral is the south transept, the main façade of which has strong vertical buttresses dividing it into three sections. The transepts were two stages high and the lower - and thus slightly earlier - windows are pointed, whilst the upper ones have round heads. This shows that at the stage of architectural history represented by the first phase of Elgin, round and pointed arches might be used almost interchangeably. A handsome doorway is set beneath a small gable between two of the buttresses. Its arch has bold dog-tooth mouldings, and the three major and two lesser capitals above the vanished shafts on each side have simple foliage carving.

Inside the transepts there was a mural passage at the upper level, opening towards the interior through arches. In the south transept, which is better preserved than the north, these arches are of alternating round and pointed form, and some of their capitals have foliage decoration of the type known as 'stiff leaf'. At the lower level on the east side of each transept was a tall shallow arch, which probably framed an altar. The south transept has an arched *piscina* (basin for washing vessels used at the altar) and aumbry (cupboard) to serve the altar, but in the north transept only the aumbry survives. On the west side of each transept was a decorative wall arcade, though this probably represents a later modification. Above the door into the south transept is a rather intriguing vesica (almond-shaped) window flanked by stone seats, which suggest that there was a timber gallery at this point. In the position corresponding to this doorway the north transept had a spiral stairway leading up to the clearstorey passage, and to a second passage which ran across the base of the roof gable. This stair would also have been the means of access to the central tower.

The nave of the first cathedral has almost entirely disappeared, but the bases of the three western piers which carried the arcades opening into the aisles remain on each side, and the lower parts of the three piers themselves survive on the south. In addition, the stubs of the inner walls of the nave stand to full height where they abut the tower. All of this shows that the nave, like the transepts, was of two storeys. At the lower level tall arches opened into the aisles, which ran the full length of the nave, and above them was a clearstorey casting light into the central space. The clearstorey incorporated a passageway between the windows on the outer face and the open arches on the inner face; it was probably similar to the upper level of windows still to be seen in the south transept.

From the lines of the aisle roof against the north-west tower it is clear that not even the

The west end of the nave. The stubs of the arcade and clearstorey can be seen at the corner of the tower (from R W Billings, Baronial and Ecclesiastical Antiquities of Scotland, Edinburgh 1845-52).

aisles of this first cathedral were covered by stone vaulting. This was rather unusual for such a magnificent building: at Glasgow Cathedral, for example, the aisles had stone vaults. However, the rather less ambitious cathedral of Brechin had no vaults and Dunblane Cathedral, as it was eventually built after various changes of design, was also denied the vaults which had been planned for its nave aisles.

The western towers

In looking at a major building a valuable pointer to the sequence of construction is the base moulding which runs around the bottom of its walls, since this was the first part of each wall to be built. From changes in the base mouldings at Elgin it may be seen that additions were made to the first design probably in the course of construction. The most important of these was the pair of towers added at the west end of the nave, which have a different base course from the transepts. Nevertheless, the decision to add them was probably taken before work on the nave was far advanced, since the western ends of the arcades were apparently built with them.

The towers rise sheer through four storeys, with strong vertical buttresses on which the stages are lightly marked by string courses (horizontal mouldings) until they are taken sharply inwards at the top stage. The lowest stage has simple lancet windows, the second stage had windows with tracery of Y-pattern, and the third stage has groupings of two pairs of openings within a single arch. A sense of lightness is given to the top stage by setting

The cathedral from the west (from R W Billings, Baronial and Ecclesiastical Antiquities of Scotland, Edinburgh 1845-52).

the single wide window on each face within a decorative arcade of three arches. The towers were probably originally intended to be capped by spires.

Internally the ground floor of each tower is covered by a stone ribbed vault, and these must have been the first such vaults to be built in the cathedral. Access to the upper floors is first by a stairway in the south tower, the steps of which have been reconstructed with gravestones. It is housed within a projection decorated externally by triplets of niches within shallow gables. This stair ascends only to the first floor, where it is covered by a delightful miniature vault, though at some date there was apparently

intermediate timber floor was inserted, which necessitated the remodelling of the windows. The lower of the two floors so formed was provided with a fireplace and a closet; it was probably occupied by one of the cathedral's officers, such as the sacrist who was responsible for the safekeeping of the cathedral's valuables .

The south-east nave chapel

A second addition to the cathedral was a chapel of three bays built in the angle between the south nave aisle and the south transept. Its construction necessitated the blocking of a window in the west wall of the transept. The arches opening into it from the aisle were carried on slender four-lobed piers; from these, transverse arches also sprang across the width of the chapel, presumably to support a timber roof. Great play was made with the way that the mouldings of the two sets of arches inter-penetrated while the capitals of the piers were also finely carved. On one of them, wyvern-like dragons play amongst the deeply undercut foliage decoration.

an intention to carry it higher. Above this level the towers each have their own staircases, and are connected by galleries at two levels below the west window. The upper floors within the towers were all originally of timber; but at a later date the first floor of the north tower had a stone barrel-vault placed over it, and an

A roof boss, from the chapter-house rebuilding of about 1500, which depicts the "arma Christi" or arms of Christ - the various items associated with his death.

The Enlargement of the Cathedral

The late thirteenth century

From the architectural evidence it is apparent that major extensions were made to the recently completed cathedral in the later thirteenth century, giving it a total length of about 85.4 m (280 ft). It is likely that the decision to enlarge was prompted by some structural reason and, although there is no contemporary record of this, there is a late medieval reference in the *Scotichronicon* to a fire in 1270. Traces of fire damage may also be seen on some of the surviving fabric.

As a result of the rebuilding thus necessitated the eastern limb was probably doubled in length as well as increased in height. In addition, broad aisles with chapels at their east ends were added along the length of the choir, leaving two bays of the new presbytery projecting free. On the

The eastern arm of the cathedral (from R W Billings, Baronial and Ecclesiastical Antiquities of Scotland, Edinburgh 1845-52).

north side of the new choir an octagonal chapter-house was added as a meeting room for the canons. At the same time the eastern bays of the nave appear to have been rebuilt and an outer line of chapels was added on each side of the nave, absorbing the three-bay chapel which had already been built on the south side. Three entrances were eventually provided into the remodelled nave. Most importantly, the great processional door between the towers was rebuilt on an impressive scale, and doorways were provided on each side of the nave to the east of the towers. That on the south was covered by a deep porch; but the northern one, with no porch, was probably a later insertion. Throughout the enlarged building, stone vaults were added over the aisles and chapels, the only exception to this being the three-bay chapel on the south side of the nave.

The choir and presbytery after 1270

Of the original eastern limb little more than the north wall was retained, and even this was badly scarred by fire. The decorative arches along its walls were cut back, leaving only the ghost of their original curves, and the wall itself was refaced, blocking the windows. The retention of this wall meant that there was no arcade opening from the canons' choir into the aisle on that side; by contrast, on the south side the wall was demolished, and an arcade of three bays was constructed. At the upper level a clearstorey was added at approximately the same height as that in the nave. But the retention of earlier work created difficulties, and the north clearstorey steps down beyond the earlier work, while there is a lack of correspondence between the two sides in the canons' choir.

The new design is seen at its best on the south side. In its two-storeyed arrangement the mason has clearly taken his lead from what survived of the nave, though he was faced with new problems because of the need to find space for a stone vault as well as a timber roof over the flanking aisles. His

The interior of the choir (from R W Billings, Baronial and Ecclesiastical Antiquities of Scotland, Edinburgh 1845-52).

solution shows some parallels with Archbishop de Grey's choir at Southwell Collegiate Church (Nottinghamshire), started in 1234. There are also parallels closer to home in the transepts of Pluscarden Priory.

At a point which probably marks the junction of the old and new work massive responds (half-piers) were constructed. These were perhaps intended to carry an arch across the main space and separate the canons' choir from the presbytery. That arch was never built; instead the responds were capped by lofty pinnacles.

The aisles and chapels flanking the new choir have been altered, but the vaults that cover them are still essentially as built after 1270. An impression of great richness is created by the complex pattern of the ribs, which include not only the structurally necessary diagonal and transverse members, but tierceron (third rank) and ridge ribs as well.

Stone vaults were not planned over the high central spaces of the cathedral. Such vaulting was extremely expensive both in materials and labour; extra support was also required to carry down to ground level the great thrusts of such an elevated mass of masonry. Elgin seems to have had an arched timber ceiling within the roof, the evidence for which may be seen in the arcs of masonry on each side of the circular window in the gable.

The east elevation (from The National Art Survey of Scotland, III, Edinburgh 1925).

The climax of the new work is the presbytery. Its western bay has the entrance from the choir aisles and the next bay is blank at the lower level because of the aisle chapels on each side. But the two narrow eastern bays project fully clear of the aisles, and their large windows must have concentrated attention of the high altar. The eastern façade, with its rows of superimposed windows belongs within a tradition of façade design stretching back to the earlier twelfth century. More specifically, the particular variant at Elgin looks back to the early thirteenth-century east front type seen for example at Whitby Abbey (Yorkshire), which has massive polygonal turrets at the angles. The design of Elgin, however, is more advanced than Whitby in having a greater number of openings at each level. But the most significant of the innovations on this façade type introduced at Elgin was the now barely detectable tracery in the lower windows: each originally contained a circlet above a small arch. The lower windows of the presbytery flanks contained a permutation on this theme in windows of two lights. It is a great loss that the tracery of the large circular window in the gable of the east façade was later rebuilt, since it would have been valuable to know how it related to the other traceried windows of the presbytery.

From the evidence of the tracery we can see that the cathedral as remodelled after 1270 must have been one of the most advanced buildings of its period in Scotland. The type of window tracery that is known as bar tracery, because of the way in which it is made up of curved bars of stone, was introduced into Scotland no earlier than the 1260s and can be seen in such buildings as Glasgow and Dunblane Cathedrals and the monasteries of Sweetheart and Pluscarden. The examples at Elgin are therefore amongst the earliest that we have.

On the south side of the presbytery are the mutilated fragments of the *sedilia*, on which the celebrant and his assistants sat at certain parts of the mass. There are four seats stepping upwards from west to east. Between the western two are fragments of one of the elaborate pinnacles which separated the arch heads; like the lower presbytery windows they were decorated with a profusion of square-flower ornament. Additional evidence for the furnishings required around an altar is to be found in the chapels at the aisle ends, each of which has a recess for a *piscina* in its south wall.

The sedilia in the south wall of the presbytery.

The chapter-house

The chapter-house was the business room of the principal clergy. In England it became quite common to construct chapter-houses of polygonal plan, and three are also known to have been built in Scotland, of which that at Elgin is one. It was entered through a small vaulted vestibule from the north aisle. The doorway from the aisle had two arches surmounted by open tracery, and the inner door was embellished by dog-tooth decoration to the jambs (sides), and with foliage carving on the capitals.

The chapter-house has been greatly altered, but it can be seen from the external traces of their arches that the original windows stretched to the full space available between the angle-buttresses. Something of the intended richness of the interior is evident from the decorative blind arcading above the entrance doorway. At the south-east corner a stairway was provided to the roof head.

The cathedral and chapter-house from the north-east. The chapter-house has been subsequently re-roofed.

The nave after 1270

The most remarkable feature of the nave after the 1270 fire was the outer row of chapels added along each side. In the later Middle Ages, as the urge for private masses to ensure salvation led to an increase of lesser altars, chapels were often added to churches in large numbers. But, except for examples at Chichester Cathedral, it was relatively unusual in Britain for this to be done as early as it was at Elgin. The windows of the new chapels appear to have been paired lancets with finely moulded jambs decorated by dog-tooth and square-flower decoration, very like those in the choir clearstorey. In their final form the chapels had individual gables, though it is uncertain if this was the original intention. Nevertheless, in the one bay where the cornice moulding of the gable survives, it does appear to be of thirteenth-century type.

It is uncertain just how much of the nave itself was rebuilt after the fire. Since some of the partly surviving eastern arcade piers were replacements it seems that the work was extensive. But the new work was carefully harmonised with what was retained, the only difference being a greater slenderness of the component parts and a tendency to increase their number. The piers which separated the outer chapels of the nave were treated as reduced versions of the new main arcade piers, except where the earlier south-east chapel was incorporated. There the earlier piers were retained to support the structure, though with new half-piers in front of them to provide additional strength.

Two bays of the south nave chapels, with tracery partly restored (from The National Art Survey of Scotland, III, Edinburgh 1925).

DETAILS OF WINDOWS ON SOUTH AISLE OF NAVE

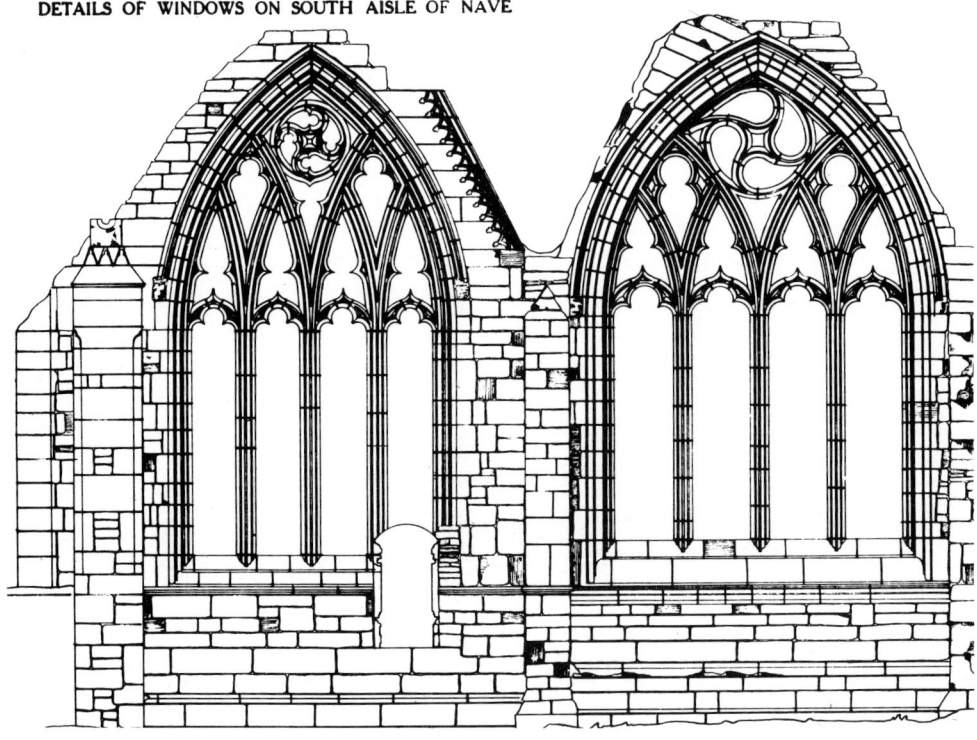

The west door (from R W Billings, Baronial and Ecclesiastical Antiquities of Scotland, Edinburgh 1845-52).

On the south side of the nave the main entrance for the lay folk was through a deep porch, lined with wall arcading above a stone bench. The doorway into the church was flanked by shafts separated by large dog-tooth decoration and supporting moulded arches. Between the doorway and the stone vault over the porch was an image niche. Within the doorway are the holes for the draw-bar by which the door could be secured from the inside.

Of an altogether more impressive scale is the great west doorway which was inserted between the two towers. It has been considerably modified by the later reconstruction of its inner skin, and the window which now surmounts it is also later, but it remains a most imposing entrance. Eight orders of engaged shafts step diagonally inwards towards the doors and carry finely moulded orders of arches, four of which were enriched by deeply undercut dog-tooth or foliage decoration. Flanking the arch of the doorway is a pair of niches for statues, and there were three further niches in the trio of gables which surmount the door. It is possible that the inspiration for this arrangement of three gables came from the late twelfth-century west doorway at Jedburgh Abbey.

Fourteenth and Fifteenth Century Repairs

The end of the 13th century and the destructions of 1390 and 1402

Once the post-1270 reconstruction was complete, Elgin Cathedral had achieved its full size. The work cannot have been long completed, however, when Scotland's peace was shattered by the outbreak of the Wars of Independence with England. A leading part in the struggle was played by Bishop David de Moravia (1299-1326), though we do not know of the cathedral having suffered as a result. Although Edward I advanced as far as Elgin in 1296 he took no action against the cathedral. Similarly, in 1336, Edward III spared the city, despite having already burnt Forres and Kinloss and preparing to do the same to Aberdeen. Nevertheless, it may be that the cathedral did suffer in some way around this time, for several decades later, Bishop Alexander Bur (1362-97) wrote to Pope Urban V asking for permission to grant indulgences to penitents who visited the cathedral on the feast of the Trinity, because it was ruinous as a result of neglect and hostile invasion.

Bishop Bur, however, was later to be faced with much greater problems as a result of the actions of Robert II's son, Alexander Stewart, earl of Buchan, also known as the Wolf of Badenoch. In 1370 Buchan had promised to defend the cathedral and its possessions, and he also served as justiciar of the North. But in 1388 he was removed from office and in 1390 it was decided that his services to the cathedral were too costly. When Bur excommunicated Buchan and turned to Thomas Dunbar, sheriff of Inverness, for protection, Buchan

An imaginary nineteenth-century view of the destruction of the cathed

descended on Elgin on 17 June 1390 and burnt the cathedral together with eighteen residences of the canons and chaplains.

Bishop Bur begged Robert III for redress, and repairs were probably started immediately though the operation was to be a protracted one. To raise funds, in 1414 the canons made an agreement that if any one of them should be elected bishop one third of the revenues of the bishopric would be devoted to the reconstruction until it was completed. By that date the cathedral had suffered further damage from an attack in 1402 by Alexander, a son of the lord of the Isles. Its position near the edge of the

1390 by the Wolf of Badenoch.

Highlands was clearly a major problem to Elgin in the later Middle Ages.

The reconstruction of the 15th and 16th centuries

The first works of repair were probably made to the eastern limb so that the main services could continue with as little interruption as possible. The quality of what was done here was very high and shows considerable sensitivity in its relationship to the existing work. The presbytery itself had probably escaped lightly, and the main alteration of which evidence remains was the insertion of new tracery into the rose window in the east gable, with a pattern of curved triangles around its perimeter.

The choir aisles and chapels appear to have required more work. Larger windows were inserted; these have intersecting tracery containing circlets, and plainly take their cue from the smaller two-light windows of the presbytery flanks. Since the tomb of Bishop John Winchester (1435-60) is placed prominently in the remodelled south chapel it might be suspected that this operation was completed while he was bishop.

Reconstruction of the central tower is said to have been carried out by Bishop John Innes (1407-14), whose tomb recorded that he was an active builder, and by his successor, Bishop Henry Lichton (1414-22). The western angles of the rebuilt tower were decorated with large niches containing the figures of a bishop and of a knight (perhaps representing

The tomb of Bishop John Winchester, who died in 1460.

the joint commitment of the clergy and the laity to the cathedral). They are now in the south-east nave chapel along with the kneeling figure of a bishop said to be from the tomb of Innes. Unfortunately the reconstruction of the tower proved to be defective, and there was a further collapse in 1506 followed by extensive rebuilding.

Reconstruction of the west front between the two towers was by Bishop Columba Dunbar (1422-34), whose arms together with those of the king and the see of Moray are on the gable. At the lowest level an inner skin of two arches was added within the processional doorway. Its arched openings had cusps (projecting spurs) at their heads and are framed by continuous bands of foliage. Between the arches is a large vesica-shaped recess which perhaps contained a representation of the Trinity, to whom the cathedral was dedicated; flanking it are adoring angels within fields of foliage. Above the doorway was inserted a vast traceried window of seven lights incorporating a great rose as the principal feature of its design. The apex of this window rises up into the gable and is surmounted by a stepped walkway, behind which the upper part of the gable is set back.

This window was not set absolutely centrally between the towers, but was nevertheless of very high calibre in both design and execution. This cannot be said for some of the later works of repair. The more complete of the two surviving

Figures of a bishop (left) and a knight (right) from the central tower, and part of an effigy thought to be from the tomb of Bishop John Innes, who died in 1414 (centre).

windows inserted in the south nave chapels, for example, has a rather uncomfortable sideways deflection in its tracery design. There are even more strikingly discordant notes in some of the windows of the remodelled chapter-house.

The chapter-house was probably one of the last parts of the cathedral to be repaired after the fire of 1390, and the arms of Bishop Andrew Stewart (1482-1501) on the central pier suggest that the work was postponed until the turn of the fifteenth and sixteenth centuries. The original window openings were reduced in size and elaborate tracery was inserted which is more remarkable for exuberance than for any sense of order. (These windows have been recently restored to provide protection for the interior of the building.) To increase its structural strength the upper walls of the chamber were internally thickened above highly enriched bands, which left enough space for the canons to sit along the original wall bench retained along its lower walls. On the north wall, however, the thickening rose above a series of five arches which gave prominence to the seats of the dean and other dignitaries of the cathedral establishment. The new vault placed over the chamber is its finest feature. It is carried on an eight-shafted central pier, at the north-western angle of which was incorporated a stone lectern carried by two strikingly sturdy angels. As part of the same building campaign a small room was added onto the east side of the vestibule; this contains a washing trough and a fireplace, and probably served as a sacristy.

The interior of the chapter-house (from R W Billings, Baronial and Ecclesiastical Antiquities of Scotland, Edinburgh 1845-52).

The Life of the Cathedral

The services

At the heart of a cathedral's life was the sequence of daily services, which was essentially similar to that evolved for monastic communities In addition there was a high mass, and usually several more masses depending on who was to be commemorated that day, while on certain days a sermon had to be preached. The performance of these services was the duty of the canons and dignitaries, though in practice much of the burden fell upon the vicars choral. Although the form of the services was relatively standardised throughout western Europe, there was still some scope for variation. At Elgin it was decided in 1242 that the model of Sarum (Salisbury) Cathedral should be followed

A depiction of a service in a major church in the fifteenth century (from a manuscript in the Musée Condé Chantilly).

"in psalmody, in reading, in singing and in all else pertaining to worship", though in the later Middle Ages a more Scottish usage would have been adopted.

A considerable number of the services were the concern of the clergy alone, and took place in the choir and presbytery. This area was therefore largely cut off from the rest of the cathedral by screens, the westernmost of which, with a central processional doorway into the choir, was given particular prominence. It was known as the rood screen because a painting or carving of the rood (crucifix) was placed above it. The main altars of the lay folk would have been placed in front of it. At Elgin the rood screen was finally destroyed only in 1640. From a description of it made then we know that the painting of the crucifixion on its west side had a pattern of stars behind it, and on the east side there was a depiction of the Last Judgement. This suggests that the upper part of the screen rose to a considerable height. There was probably a gallery (known as the rood loft) above the lower part of the screen and the paintings on wooden panelling would have risen above this.

The stalls of the canons would have extended along the flanks of the choir in front of the screens between the piers, and would have turned at right-angles against the rood screen. The more prominent stalls for the bishop and dignitaries were placed at the ends of the stalls, and a second row of stalls for the vicars would have been set in front of those of the canons. In the later Middle Ages stalls tended to become more elaborate and to be surmounted by canopies both to give them greater prominence and shelter from draughts. It can be seen that the great respond (half-pier) on the south side of the choir, where the bishop's throne is likely to have been, has been cut back to accommodate a loftier piece of furnishing than was originally intended.

Monuments within the cathedral

A cathedral was the usual place of burial for its bishops and for the great layfolk of the diocese. Elgin still has a fine series of tombs, though it is now impossible to be certain for whom many of them were made. One tomb was an integral part of the presbytery design and appears likely to have been provided by Bishop Archibald (1253-98) for his own eventual use. The effigy which used to lie below the cinquefoiled (five-lobed) arch is

The tomb in the north wall of the presbytery, possibly made for Bishop Archibald.

gone, but the architectural details of the steeply angled gable which embraced both the arch and an image niche are still well preserved.

In the bay to the west of this are the fragments of a very ambitious tomb. It almost filled the arch from the north aisle into the presbytery, and was once capped by three steeply pointed and richly ornamented gables separated by miniature pinnacles. One of the gables covered the doorway that allowed access between aisle and presbytery, and the other two corresponded to the wider arch covering the now-destroyed tomb chest and its effigy.

The chapel on the south side of the presbytery is dominated by the splendid tomb of Bishop John Winchester (1435-60) which is the most complete in the cathedral. The bishop is shown in his mass vestments, laid out on a tomb chest which has an arcaded front below an elaborate ogee (double-curved) arch. The inscription may be translated: "Here lies John Winchester, lord bishop of Moray, of distinguished memory, who died on the 20th day of the month of April in the year of the Lord 1460". This, like most tombs, would once have been finely painted, and traces of the angels that were shown surrounding him in death are still to be seen on the underside of the canopy. In the centre of the chapel is a tomb chest of interest for the secular dress of its effigy. Its inscription may be translated: "Here lies the noble and powerful Lord Alexander Gordon, first earl of Huntly, lord of Gordon and Badenoch, who died at Huntly, 15 July in the year of the Lord 1470".

In the aisle to the west of this chapel is a rectangular frame enclosing a tomb recess. Within this recess is an effigy of a bishop, dressed in mass vestments, which is clearly too small to belong here. Although the royal arms of Scotland and those of the diocese appear on the sides of the small canopy that frames his head the identity of this bishop is unknown. In the centre of the aisle, but no longer in its original position, is a secular effigy in armour. The inscription records: "Here lies William de le Hay, sometime lord of Lochloy, who died the 8th day of the month of December in the year of the Lord 1422, for whose soul may the Lord be propitiated".

The south transept has two mural canopied tombs against its south wall, both of which contain effigies of knights. The eastern of these however, must originally have been the tomb of Bishop James Stewart (1460-62), since his arms are on the canopy. The effigy bears the arms of the Innes family and may represent Robert Innes of Invermarkie. It has not so far been possible to identify who was commemorated by the tomb to its west, the construction of which necessitated the narrowing of the adjacent doorway.

There are also two tombs with effigies in the north transept, but these have lost the canopies that surmounted them. One effigy appears to have been in secular dress but is unidentifiable. The other figure, a knight, bears the arms of the Dunbar family on his breastplate.

There is another group of memorials in the chapter-house. These were originally set up in the parish church of St Giles for a number of post-Reformation bishops of the diocese and their families. These bishops had used the parish church as their cathedral after the simpler services of the reformed Church had reduced the need for such complex buildings as the medieval cathedral. The memorials were moved to the chapter-house when the parish church was rebuilt in 1827-8.

The two tombs in the south transept.

The cathedral chanonry

The cathedral did not stand alone; around it were many other buildings, including the residences of the canons, dignitaries and vicars. All of these were set within a stout encircling wall pierced by four gateways. A fragment of this wall survives within a modern housing estate to the south-east of the cathedral and its massive scale shows that defence was a serious matter. There is also a surviving gateway, known as Panns Port; but it was not one of the main entrances to the chanonry. It has suffered from being "improved" by the addition of fake battlements and loop-holes, but the provision for both a portcullis and doors shows that it was meant to be strong.

Panns Port, one of the gates into the cathedral precinct.

Within the wall the manses of the canons would have stood each within its own garden. The manses of the prebendaries of Duffus and Unthank survived until 1840 before being demolished, while that of Inverkeithny is absorbed within a later house. But one of the largest of the manses still stands in a fragmentary state and, as such, is the best example of a canon's manse in Scotland. Known misleadingly as the 'Bishop's House', it was more likely the residence of the precentor, and its design shows that canons might live in a tower-house similar to those occupied by wealthy lairds.

The house is not at present open to visitors, but may be viewed from the outside. The main body was a rectangle, with its principal room, the hall, raised to first-floor level above a vaulted basement, which included the kitchen. On the upper floor were lesser chambers, and there would have been garrets in the roof space. At the north-east corner of the main block was a square stair tower, beyond which was a smaller second block, with two floors of private chambers above a vaulted basement. This rather complex plan was perhaps the result of more than one building campaign. Much of the work, however, is of 1557, to judge by an inscription on the gable of the stair turret; and the decoration of the building included the arms of Bishop Patrick Hepburn (1538-73). Also built into the side of the house is a plaque with the arms of Alexander Lyon, precentor between 1527 and 1540, and of Robert Reid, bishop of Orkney (1541-58), who had earlier been subdean of the cathedral (1524-29) and official of the diocese (1527-30).

Later History

Reformation and after

The Reformation Parliament of 1560 abolished the mass and rejected the pope's authority over the Scottish Church. It now proved to be the cathedral's misfortune that it had not served as a parish church, for whereas several of Scotland's cathedrals wholly or partly survived the Reformation because they were still required for public worship, at Elgin the bishops simply moved to the parish church. Although Bishop Patrick Hepburn (1538-73) did offer to contribute towards the cathedral's repair in 1569, it is doubtful if he had much interest in it.

The cathedral soon began to suffer from the changed attitudes towards it. In 1561 Lord James Stewart may have purged it of its "popish" trappings, and in 1567-8 the Privy Council ordered the removal of its lead roofing, probably because the more acquisitive among the local population had already started doing so. The lead and bells were probably destined for sale in the Netherlands, but the ship carrying these commodities and others from Aberdeen Cathedral was so overladen that it foundered in Aberdeen harbour.

There was some change of attitude in 1569 when the Privy Council ordered the roofs to be re-covered, but it is unlikely that action was taken. Nevertheless, the north-east of Scotland was a conservative area and a public mass was celebrated in the cathedral in 1594 after the battle of Glenlivet, at which the Catholic earl of Huntly defeated the Government forces of the earl of Argyll. It is also said to have been the scene of both

The cathedral in the late seventeenth century, before the collapse of the central tower (from John Slezer, Theatrum Scotiae, 1693).

Catholic and Protestant worship well into the 17th century. But such limited use could not reverse the damage done by the removal of the roof's lead covering, and on 4 December 1637 the choir roof blew down in a gale. Human actions also played a part, as in 1640 when the minister of the parish, together with the lairds of Innes and Brodie, broke up the rood screen for firewood; its painted decoration was then still plainly visible. The greatest single disaster in the cathedral's decline was the collapse of the central tower on Easter Sunday of 1711, taking a great part of the nave with it. The only part of the structure which received some care was the chapter-house, which was used as a meeting room for the Elgin incorporated trades.

Modern attitudes to the cathedral

The decay of the cathedral was halted only in the early nineteenth century, when medieval architecture was coming to be increasingly appreciated. Following the final abolition of bishops in the Church of Scotland in 1689 the cathedral had technically become the property of the Crown, but it was local initiative which first saw the need for action. In 1807 John Shanks was appointed keeper of the cathedral with the job of looking after it and showing it to visitors, and he single-handedly cleared out the ruins to reveal much that was previously unknown. In 1816 and 1820, the Crown was asked for assistance in this great work, and eventually it was accepted that it had the leading role to play. Robert Reid, the King's architect in Scotland, prepared reports on works required to stabilise the fabric in 1824 and 1834, and a grant was made towards Shanks's salary. Improvements were also made to the setting of the cathedral by the removal of houses which approached it too closely and by the construction of an enclosing wall. The view of the east front was enhanced by the removal of a brewery complex and the provision of a sunken wall. Much of this was done in a co-operative endeavour between the Office of Works and the Burgh of Elgin.

The eastern limb of the cathedral in 1826 (from A Series of Views ... of Elgin Cathedral).

The preservation of the cathedral has, however, posed major problems since much of the stone of which it is built is prone to rapid decay. Several operations have already been necessary to replace stone that is so weathered as to threaten the stability of the fabric. In undertaking this work Historic Scotland attempts to ensure that the historical and architectural integrity of the fabric is in no way compromised. Where badly damaged carved and moulded stones can be replaced by faithful copies of what was there, this is done. Where there is any element of doubt the stone is simply blocked out in a way that will not detract from the appearance of the structure, but avoids conveying a false message. In addition, all areas of new stone are carefully dated so that students of the cathedral's architecture need never be in any doubt as to whether they are looking at authentic or replica work.

By such means it is hoped that this most beautiful structure can be passed on to future generations as it has come down to us, and that it will continue to provide an inspirational pointer to the architecture, faith and history of those who built it.

Further Reading

D MacGibbon and T Ross	*The Ecclesiastical Architecture of Scotland*, 3 vols (Edinburgh 1896-97), 2, 121-145.
R G Cant	*Historic Elgin and its Cathedral* (Elgin 1974).
D Omand (ed)	*The Moray Book* (Edinburgh 1976).
R Fawcett	*Scottish Medieval Churches* (Edinburgh 1985).
S Cruden	*Scottish Medieval Churches* (Edinburgh 1986).

View of the cathedral precinct and Panns Port from the south-east.
(Reproduced by kind permission of the National Gallery of Scotland, Department of Prints and Drawings)